THE BANISHMENT
OF KALIYA

THE BANISHMENT

OF KALIYA

As told in the form of a narrative
poem in English

By Henry C. Timm

Foreword by
Graham M. Schweig, Ph.D.

Preface by Steven J. Rosen

Caravaggio Press
Sturgeon Bay, WI

For further information contact

Caravaggio Press

500 N 9th Ct Unit 213

Sturgeon Bay, WI 54235

Phone (920) 818-0921

*This poetic version of The Banishment of Kaliya
is gratefully dedicated to my son, Radhavallabha
Das, whose joyful energy happily drew the
Krishna stories to my attention.*

THE BANISHMENT

OF KALIYA

CONTENTS

FOREWORD

Across all cultures and across the millennia,
humans have delighted in telling and re-telling
stories. As such stories are passed down through
the generations, they take on new life in their fresh
renditions. No matter how grand or intimate an
event a story may relate, such stories tell us who we
are as humans. In a very real sense, all of humanity
is represented, even if just in a small way, in every
story.

Our storyteller here, Henry Timm, offers us
a fresh rendition of an ancient tale. It is very well-
known story from an ancient scriptural text
originally in the Sanskrit language appearing in
sacred India that is at least two millennia old. It is
known as the Bhāgavata Purāṇa, or "the ancient
stories (purāṇa) about the divine (bhāgavata)." This

sacred writing is one of the most beloved in all of India and among Hindu traditions, especially because it presents the stories that reveal the divinity of Krishna along with those personages who are intimately and lovingly (bhakti) connected to him.

The "Banishment of Kaliya" is an especially popular story, though just one among many such beloved stories from the Bhāgavata Purāṇa. As with most stories, there are certain common elements: there is a hero, who is Krishna himself, who is helped by those who are devoted to him while others pose as adversaries. Typically in stories, the hero takes up a task, and is committed to a purpose, and such a purpose reaches fulfillment by the end of the story.

What stands out here is the way that Henry Timm brings out this ancient story from the Sanskrit and retells it in English, and renders it in rhyming rhythmic verse that reflects something of the spirit or ethos of the original—for Krishna is known to be that divine hero, that supreme divinity in whom one discovers all that is supremely beautiful, playful, and delightful. We are now fortunate to have before us the rendition of a story that truly reflects something of these three qualities that are themselves embedded in the very story itself.

Graham M. Schweig, Ph.D.
Professor of Religion
Christopher Newport University, Virginia
Author-Translator of *Bhagavad Gita: The Beloved Lord's Secret Love Song*

PREFACE

"You have to know the past
to understand the present."
— Carl Sagan

We often mistakenly view the past with a modern lens. In literary and historical analysis, such a flawed view is called "presentism," i.e., the anachronistic use of present-day ideas in an attempt to interpret the past. This is rightly seen as a form of cultural bias, in which we inadvertently distort history based on modern preconceptions. But, sometimes, there is an entirely different dynamic at play, where the past calls out to us in no uncertain terms, attempting to enlighten us according to universal and abiding truths, hinting at a reality that, indeed, currently engulfs us all.

We are in the midst of a crisis, with environmental and ecological concerns that would have been difficult to anticipate by ancient man. Climate change, pollution, species extinction. Time, we are told, is running out, as we leave the world our frightening carbon footprints, with shadowy steps our descendants dare not follow. This worldwide phenomenon has even affected the Yamunā, the river at the heart of the story you are about to read. She has suffered as a result. Bathing in her sacred waters is no longer possible.

Contemporary scholars, such as David Haberman and Shrivatsa Goswami, see in the Kāliya narrative an ancient warning for a modern problem. The serpent in our story had poisoned the entire region, devastating its water, land, animals and birds. It is clear that a facsimile of Kāliya's poison endangers us even now, manifesting as selfishness, exploitation of natural resources, and the subtle industrial wastes that pour into the river of our lives. It is equally clear that, like Krishna, we must react to ecological defilement, attempting to save the world from the serpent of exploitation. We must defeat the modern-day Kāliya once and for all.

If the poetic narrative in this small volume helps to instill a sense of moral duty, in which we take responsibility for the pollution of our world, we ipso facto become part of an urgent restoration process. The prototype is Krishna's overwhelming success in the Kāliya story: By his joyful dance, Garuḍa and Kāliya go back to their respective lakes; the gopas and gopīs are rejuvenated; and all the creatures and natural assets of the Earth are restored to their healthy state once again. Krishna steps in to save the day. Even though the serpent tries to crush Krishna in his coils, goodness overcomes evil, trampling all darkness under his dancing lotus feet. Let us allow those divine feet to do their work yet again.

Steven J. Rosen
Senior Editor of the *Journal of Vaishnava Studies*
Author of *Śrī Chaitanya's Life and Teachings: The Golden Avatāra of Divine Love* (Lexington Books)

DRAMATIS PERSONAE

Balarama – The elder brother of Krishna
Bhagavan – Another name for Vishnu or Krishna, meaning the supreme
Garuda – The eagle carrier for Lord Vishnu
Gopas – Cowherd boys of Vrindavana
Gopis – Cowherd girls of Vrindavana
Govinda – Another name of Krishna, meaning protector of the cows
Kalendi – A lake that formed off the river Yamuna
Kaliya – The name of a many-headed serpent
Krishna – The Supreme Lord in human form
Nanda – The father of Krishna
Pariksit (or Maharaj Pariksit) – The listener of the tale, an emperor cursed to die in seven days
Ramanaka – The land Kaliya was from
Shaubhare – A sage who meditated in the water and thus became a friend to the fish
Shuka (or Shri Shuka) – The speaker of the tale
Vishnu – The Supreme Lord
Vraj – The land where Krishna spend his childhood
Vrinda – Short for Vrindavana, the land where Krishna spend his childhood
Yamuna (or Yamuna-devi) – The river that runs through Vraj
Yashoda – The mother of Krishna

I. KRISHNA COMES TO
THE RIVER YAMUNA

"So, with the killing of the donkey demon Dhenuka, Krishna and Balarama returned home to resume their pampered lives in the land of Vraj." And with those words, Shri Shuka the sage brought the telling of his story to its end.

The sage took a deep breath.

The Maharaj Pariksit leaned forward. His eyes were as wide as a child's and he looked like he was about to fall into the sudden silence that had arisen between Shri Shuka and himself. With his hands fluttering in the air the Maharaj said "And so? And so?"

Shri Shuka frowned. "And so what, oh Great One?" he asked.

The Maharaj frowned and said, "Is that all? Is that the end for now?"

Shri Shuka smiled and took another deep breath and said, "By no means, oh Noble Listener for hearing about Lord Krishna and reciting His achievements are the means to purification." Then he bowed his head and chanted to himself until the beginning image of the new story appeared in his mind. As this happened, he thanked his beloved Krishna, looked up at the Maharaj and with a broad new smile said, "We will now hear the story of Kaliya, the seven headed snake who poisoned the River Yamuna and how Krishna banished him and purified Yamuna River and its Lake Kalendi once again."

The Maharaj returned the sage's smile, leaned back, folded his hands over the perfect circumference of his waist, closed his eyes and said, "Proceed indeed, for this is an adventure that I find particularly pleasing."

Shri Shuka then began:
So wandered Krishna Lord through Vrinda wood
with friends and brother – when his brother could–
until one day, with Balarama gone,
Lord Krishna to Kalendi came and stood.

His friends and He gaped wide eyed! All along
the strand lay many gopas in a throng
as still as death. The herd was dead there too
and those with Bhagavan cried "Lord, what's wrong?

And Krishna said:
"Look how they knelt so ordered fro and to,
to drink and quench their thirst as all would do,
but here, this water is a poisonous swill
and they were overwhelmed, too soon to rue

the need that drove them to this baneful kill."
Seeing those who called him "Master" laid so ill,
Lord Krishna looked and bathed them with his eyes.
The nectar of his gaze brought life to fill

each heart and mind, each hand and arm and thigh,
each man and beast brought back to laugh and sigh.

They rose and stood amazed in sight and breath
and spoke of how they drank and fell to die,
and how Govinda looked upon their strife
and with his gaze brought all through death to life.

But Krishna, Lord of Laughter, Lord of Light
Thought how to purge Yamuna, set it right.
For knowing how and why Kaliya came,
He knew as well . . . .

II. PROLOGUE

But suddenly, the Maharaj called "Stop!"
His hand shot in the air, one finger raised as if to
prod the very blanket of the stars. "Oh, Noble
Sage," he wailed, "forgive my turtle mind. You know
that I must hear things one by one. The integers
must come before the sum to such as I. Your telling
is too swift," he said.

"Too swift?" the sage replied.

"Indeed!" the Maharaj said, "If you could
just back up a little; remind us how that monster,
Kaliya, got to Yamuna in the first place."

"Ah," the Sage said with a nod. "Yes, that is
very important."

The Maharaj shook his head up and down in
agreement and resumed his listening pose.

Shri Suka smiled once again . . . and then
went on to add a belated prologue to his tale.

As you well know, oh wisest king of man,
Lord Vishnu rides upon an eagle's back.
The bird, Garuda, King of Eagle Clan
Can see the world as either food... or not!

Yamuna River feeds Kalendi Lake,
the river and the lake both deep and wide,
were pure, so pure they favored with a yield
Twice rich with fish – Garuda's favorite meal.

One day Garud' was gliding on the wind
to scan the waves and water down below
To find one fish – a fish of royal hue.
And when he did, he claimed that fish his due.

He skimmed the waves and teased them with his claws.
His talons tickled up the fish's back.
That royal fish gave him a merry chase
Until he snatched that beauty; ate it raw!

Now, this poor fish was more than simply fish.
He was a tribal prince, a scaly thing
beloved of his clan, all they could wish,

now to them lost, their king mere memory.

But near that lake, there lived a sage alone.
Shaubhare; in whose thoughts wisdom prevailed.
To him the fish would come to tell their woes.
And so they came again and wept and wailed

and that same sage rose up and shook his fist.
"That hungry bird has heard my words before!
I've told him, 'Leave this water folk alone.
Dine ye on snails! Or better yet, eat snakes!

If he comes back and feeds upon these fish
or even takes a scale to pick his teeth,
Such is enough to forfeit life: his own!
And so this law shall stand as fast as stone!"

So Lake Kalendi, since that day 'til now
Has seen the last of this Garuda's brow.
And so it was and always was to be
And yet the eagle's stomach spoke, you see.
"Where shall I go and where now shall I feed?"
Then he remembered from his wandering
There was a place called Ramanaka Weald

Where many worshiped snakes, of all such things.

And this is where Kaliya made his home ~
yes, he of many heads and sharpened fangs
who poison through each orifice could hurl ~
that was his world, his see and his domain.

So there the folk left offerings for this snake.
And even snakes they offered, which he ate.
They brought the snakes and left the snakes behind
and never thought, "He feeds on his own kind!"

Kaliya didn't care; he'd eat the world!
And when the world was done, he'd eat the moon,
and then upon the planets he would feast
and finish off his dinner with the sun.

And if the people stopped to bring him gifts,
He'd feed upon their lives, their dreams, the churl;
all seasoned with the poison in his mind
and heart that kept him bloated, all the time.
So, when Garuda came at first to feast
upon the food so often left to please
the monster... well, folks thought and then they said,

"Bon Appetite! Why leave this snake our gifts

When Vishnu's eagle holds a stronger sway?
Let him receive our offerings, day by day."
Kaliya, with his many, many eyes
saw how the eagle came to take his food
and with his many tongues he told himself,
"This will not do; these gifts are meant for me!"
And then his mouth would water, don't you see?
He waited for the offerings to be made

and swept them up the moment they were laid
and let Garuda feast as best he might.
Garuda, though, was not about to fade
and shy away to hunt in glen or glade

and look for mice and covet what that snake~
one head or many heads ~ would try to take.
"I, after all, take Vishnu on my back,"
he argued loud enough for all to hear.
"I soar the world with Majesty astride
my shoulders and between my lofty wings.
I hear the very song that God will sing!
Who does this belly crawler think he is

To filch the gifts so sweetly left for me?
And then, to make these matters muchly worse,
it's his own kind he eats! He's just a curse!"
Garuda searched the lake; the serpent found

and called him to the justice that he vowed.
His call embraced and shook the tops of trees.
His wingspan nearly circled all the seas.
His talons ripped the shadows like the sun,

but none of this caused Kudra's son to quake.
Kaliya raised his heads; his eyes turned red
as smelting coals that shape the waxing blade.
His fangs all glistening glimmered into light

the darkening pit that formed his open maws,
as poison dripped from fang to fang to smite
Garuda's white and golden feathered throat.
Garuda soared, then spread his talons wide
then seemed to loose his wind, fail to the left
then taken by a down draft, shrieked a cry . . .

Kaliya hisssed. Tongues flickering side to side,
He licked his lipsss and charged the falling bird.

Garuda tipped his right wing up, away
and lowered his left ~ it shone like lustering gold ~

and struck the forest of heads a typhoon blow
that shuddered deep into the serpent's lungs
and whispered through the poison in his veins,
"Where can I go to get away from thisss?"

Then he remembered what none other knew.
"Shaubhare made a sanctuary place,
a place Garuda must not ever go:
Kalendi, where Yamuna River flows."

And to Yamuna, there he stole that day,
he and his wives and sons and poisoned ways,
to make his safety where none else were safe:
Which brings us back where Krishna us awaits.

III. HOW KRISHNA
CLEANSED THE LAKE

So saying, Shri Shuka smiled; and Pariksit
too. The latter liked an ordered world with things
all in a row – no gardens wild, no hidden vines, no
shadowy murky beauty in his realm for in the best
of worlds, order makes a beauty all its own and
order's beauty is a thing for all to see. And that is
about as clearly as any of his thoughts ever came
out which is why he so loved hearing stories like
this one.

"So," Shri Shuka said, "have I then slacked
your thirst for first things first at last?"

"And nicely too; now on to greater things,"
Pariksit said. He laughed and clapped his hands,
then folded them across his lap and leaning
towards the sage, he said, "Proceed."

Shri Shuka took a deep breath ~ collecting
his thoughts as he did so ~ and went on gladly
towards the heart of the tale.

From that first moment when the serpent came,
Yamuna-devi doubled up in pain
and seized her belly like it was on fire
and burned all black and red, all guilt and shame.

"Why She?" you ask, 'twas not her sin that washed
upon the banks and killed all living things.
But sin will taint the world, stain each and all;
a wretched flood fed by a cancerous rain.

Kaliya's venom spread, reached out, rose higher
like oily fingers dancing in a geyer.
The river boiled, fumes choked the sacred air.
Birds on the wing breathed death, fell to the mire.

Waves rose and coughed and burned the beaches there.
In yellow light they bruised. The trees went bare.
Deep down, the serpent dreamed, safe and secure
and never gave a whit, nor thought to care.
Nor did he on the day the gopas came

and out of desperate thirst, they drank his swill
and fell into a death and lay there still.
Lord Krishna called them back, each name by name.

Then each one smiled, felt life alive and sure
flow through his body, limbs all fresh and pure,
and sang Govinda's praise from earth to sky
and danced His Grace, His Beauty and Allure.

So Krishna laughed and danced as well; leapt high
and landing low brought light from brow to thigh,
then stopped and stared and motioned to a tree ~
the one lone, tall kadamba, green, alive.

And Krishna said:
"Now who can tell how that tree there can breathe;
how life can flow from root to limb to leaf?"
No one could say. They shrugged to hear the word.
"Lord Vishnu blessed its life to wait for me!"
And straightway to the tree and like a bird
from limb to limb the topmost limb secured,
He flexed his limbs and stretched, both left and right;
drew tight his belt and called and then they heard:

"Keep watch for this should be a jolly sight."
He loosed his hair and tied it good and tight
and slapped his chest and danced upon the limb.
"No demon can withstand my loving might."

He leapt and laughed and down and down he skimmed,
a bird to water born, so lithe and slim.
His friends could hear him smile and sing his best.
His slender body glowed its joyful hymn.

His lotus fingers touched the putrid crest
and played the lake like sitars to protest
the sleeping serpent, who woke up to meet
the awful tune announcing his new guest.

Lord Krishna, with his glowing arms then beat
the waves so that his raga was complete.
"No more of this," the waking monster roared.
"Who is this latest imp I must defeat?"
But Krishna played right on, his music soared,
played on his skin and silken clothes the more
until Kaliya whined to stop the sound,
the wrath of beauty flooding sea and shore.

"No more! These liquid fingers must be bound.
No more! This languid torso turning round
and round and round . . . these lotus blossom feet."
So, round and round, Kaliya coiled and wound

the dancer to his serpent flesh and beat
the air about his head and bared his teeth
and bit against Lord Krishna's heart and breast
to stop the noise and save his poisoned peace.

The gopas moaned in terror and distress.
Lord Krishna was their world, their hopes, their best
of each and all, their wives, their wealth, their joy.
They fell to earth, tore hair and beat their chests.

Those working in the fields soon heard the roil
and came to see what further grief would spoil
the world. And even cattle came to see,
and stood, wide eyed, feared even to recoil.

So too did omens show in numbers three.
The earth did quake and tremble, stones fell free.
And stars likewise burned through the living sky
and eyelids trembled so 'twas hard to see.

Then in the village, children stopped their play
where Nanda and Yashoda made their day.
"What thing is this that stops the running hours?"
Cried Nanda to Yashoda, "Who can say?"

Yashoda held her breath. "The dark devours
the light," poor Nanda cried. "Look to those flowers!
They wilt and shudder, shrivel to the ground."
Yashoda shook her head and darkly glowered

to find Govinda's brother. Not a sound
'til crafty Balarama had been found.
"Now Balarama, where did Krishna go?"
"Out with the gopas; are they not around?"

"Oh dreadful omens! One and all, come show!
Is Krishna live or dead? We need to know.
"Take hands now, each to each. Look for their tracks."
All spoke at once, the mystery to behold.

The omens came mid-day; all left their food,
their drinks, their business, gossip and their jobs
and, young and old, all gathered as they could
and held their breaths and throttled back their sobs.

"See here, these tracks, these footprints surely show
the way to Krishna. Here ~ a lotus flower
and there, a barley corn . . . and now a goad . . .
here is a flag . . . a lightening bolt . . . a flower . .

Again and all the others, one then two
then three and then again, they saw the clues ~
Yashoda, Nanda, neighbors, all as one,
and Balarama too ~ just for the fun.
Then suddenly the shock, the frightful sight
before them in the lake! A hue and cry
rose up for Krishna trapped from chin to thigh
and there the serpent coiled to end their fight.

Wherefore this misery; wherefore and why?
Forgetting who He was, was He to die?
Just might the monster win, devour their trust,
turn all their joy and hope into a lie?

Then Balaram' turned up to find the fuss.
He saw what they were seeing and beyond
and knew full well just who his brother was;
laughed to himself, bent down and picked a frond

still growing near the bless'd kadamba tree
and found a pleasant rock to sit upon
and watch his brother show'r transcendency
like golden gee from Heaven flowing down.

But oh, the scene around him that he saw!
The cowherd boys had fainted all away.
Not one of them could speak; not one could say
How Krishna came so near the serpent's maw!
The younger gopis moaned and held their breaths,
heard echoes of his lovely words again
but saw his tender smiles eclipsed by death,
saw stars go blind, burn off like desert rain.

Yashoda stood with mothers like herself,
embraced his silent danger with her heart
while others who recalled the sacred elf
made whispered lit'nies of his playful art.

The older men, like Nanda and the rest
who lived for Krishna, swore his trust to keep,
resolved to end their lives, began the press
to cast themselves into Kalendi's deep.
But Balarama stood and spread his arms

and came between these fathers and the flood.
"Hold back! You must not do yourself such harm.
Care for the boy as duty says you should.

"I know how much he lives within your hearts;
how much his joy makes fresh the air you breathe;
how he turns rain to nectar with his arts;
but don't forget what else he can achieve.
"Take heed and heart and cease this 'Mercy me,
what will we do without him in our midst?
Be patient with his strength. Just wait and see
his power blossom forth and then persist.

"His grace, so like a pearl deep in the sea,
bewilders all with his dark mystery,
then glows like dawn, thanks to his rich prowess,
to those surrendered souls brings happiness."

And all this time ~ about and hour or so ~
the Lord pretended he was merely man.
But seeing how his folk were brought so low,
thought, "Now it's time to end this, and I can."

So, first he smiled to all those on the strand
and with that smile he then began to grow
and stroking poor Kaliya with his hand
said, "There are things about me you should know.

"You see me as a little cow-herd boy
but surely you have greatness to behold,
but greatness born of love and sacred joys
is greater great than great and bolder bold."
By then Kaliya's skin was stretching tight ~
Young Krishna grew beyond his weakening grasp. ~
and with a roar, released the laughing mite
and rose to face him like a giant asp.

Not only one, but many poisoned heads
began to sway and dart with forkéd tongues,
began to flicker death. Govinda knew
the double danger; well he understood.

But that was play to Krishna, fact enough
for him to laugh and sing, sashay and prance,
turn somersaults, do splits and show his stuff
and teach Kaliya what it means to dance.

He circled round the serpent left to right
and everywhere Kaliya tried to strike,
the boy was somehow "else" and out of sight
then back again as slick as melting ice.

Now was the time to put his friends at peace.
His lotus smile brought joy back to their hearts.
And just to show the power of his reach,
he danced to show the meaning of all arts.

Up high he reached to lower Kaliya's crown.
He leaped upon his head, then shook a leg.
His lotus feet were flashing up and down.
Kaliya felt the joy and moaned to beg

the Master of all Arts to stop. But no,
Lord Krishna leaped from crown to crown and sang.
The gopis blushed to see him dancing so.
His song of joy from earth to heaven rang.

Those lotus feet began to blossom red
as Krishna touched the gems Kaliya wore.
But on he danced and sang from head to head
as his performance toward the heavens soared.

There, all the angels, once they over-heard,
came rushing to the scene to join the song.
And just to know all heav'n should get the word,
they brought their holy instruments along.
Then what a sound! The cosmos echoed clear
with sitars, zithers, tablas and their kind.
That raucous beauty echoed on the wind
as stars and planets wept, such joy to hear.

So was the snake chastised with pure delight
and flowers and gifts and songs fell from above.
His poison turned against him, burned his plight
from skin to bone; his death drew near from love.

So near his angry heart began to surge.
He vomited red blood from nose and mouth,
from head to head. As one would rise and lurch,
Lord Krishna danced it down again to purge
all wickedness from this poor creature's core;
all wickedness there was and even more.

Kaliya roared and wept and from his eyes
more poison poured 'till he was weeping clear.
And when he tried to raise a head to sigh,

Lord Krishna danced it down with joy severe.

And every time another head bowed down,
more flowers fell from heaven, round and round.
As one by one, his many heads went dumb,
through all that dark he slowly saw his fear

of light approach and knew his death would come.
He saw Garuda, flying low and fast
and knew him as Lord Vishnu's bird at last.
Then Vishnu, Lord himself, broke into sight.

Kaliya gasped as dark turned into light
and finally showed the Lord he thought a boy.
He understood and wept a final tear
to know that he'd been battling with pure Joy.

And as that light within his spirit rose,
his eyelids, one by one, began to close.
Kaliya's wives stood by and watched it all,
knew well what weight withstood Kaliya's sin.

Lord Krishna was the master of his fall
and bears the weighty universe within.

Those light and lotus feet bore heavy heels.
Their husband well deserved the death they brought.

No god-head ever lived within his heart;
no world but empty darkness ever sought.
But on Kaliya's breath, so faint a sigh . . .
in words they never knew he understood
until they saw that glimmer in his eye,
and knew he would have said them if he could.

'Twas then they rent their garments, tore their hair;
remembered how Eternity is now,
that just one moment in a life, though rare,
could open to the universe, show how
Lord Krishna lives in every new drawn breath
and breathes all life to quell and conquer death.

Their children led them where Lord Krishna stood.
And there the wives fell down and wept their woe
and begged the Lord of Creatures, sweet and good,
to liberate and shield their husband's soul.

IV. KALIYA'S WIVES
PRAY FOR KALIYA'S REDEMPTION
(The Faith Sonnets)

FIRST THEY OFFER PRAISE TO KRISHNA

The Wives:
Oh Noble One, here once upon a time
appears a child, so full of tricks and all
that laughter was the rhythm of his rhyme
as he will play with ropes and butter balls.

And Noble One, then will a lover come,
a youth of virile grace and noble thigh
to charm and woo them all and every one
Who falls within the blessing of his eye.

Then comes the day when all will hail a king
unlike all other rulers of this earth.
He comes to trample evil, heal the sting
of death and show such passing as new birth.

His name is Bhagavan, Govinda, Heaven's Joy,
One Krishna, All in One, The Holy Boy.

THEN THEY PRAY FOR KALIYA'S REDEMPTION

The Wives:
Oh Lord of Heav'n and all the glorious throng,
we pray You heard, that moment unto death;
at last, Your Name. It shimmered like a song
and begged Your holy promise; his last breath.

Of all the sweet things of this bitter life
Your love breaks down the dam of cruel hate,
smooths out the roar and trembling of all strife,
but for Kaliy', his umbrage held so late . . .

Until that breath we know his soul was blind.
We know all love went by the board with him
until your dance brought vision to his mind.
Breathe in Your breath that he may breathe again.
Krishna:
No breath is lost that whisper's faith so new.
No vision blind if his last breath be true.

NOW THEY PRAY FOR KRISHNA'S MERCY

The Wives:
Oh Lord of Light, of Justice and of Hope,
A breath ago we'd let Kaliya be
for we were weary, each and all to cope
with such an anger, wide as all the sea.

But see him low; see how he suffers now,
no thought of life, his senses all a-swirl;
his bowed and bloody heads, his bleeding brows.
He is a broken thing. You rule the world.

How great You are; how small he has become
but now he dreams Your Name, so all is new.

Think how much sweet devotion he could sing
in every wave and every drop of dew.

Krishna:
So do I sing the Song and string the Bow,
And lathe each mind and body into Soul.

Narrator:
So Bhagavan released the broken beast.

V. KALIYA REDEEMED

Kaliya slowly woke, came back to sense;
bowed down his heads to show his lowly state
and spoke to Krishna in a softened voice.

"This universe is ordered by your vows,
as many natures as your law allows.
We serpents are a cranky lot, you know.
How can we change, your blessed peace to show?

If you can change us, Lord, that would be best,
but even in chastisement, we are blessed."
Then Bhagavan, love lighting up his face,
said to Kaliya, "You must leave this stream;
give humans and their cattle respite here.
Those mortals who remember this command
and chant it both at dawn and dusk each day

will cease to fear you; leave you well alone.

Henceforth, this is a sacred bathing strand.
Who bathes with me in mind is freed from sin.
And you who left your first home out of fear,
came here to wear your anger on your face,
are now made whole; I've danced away your pain.
You need not fear Garuda e're again."

So freed, Kaliya, sons and wives and friends,
all worshiped Krishna from day's dawn 'till end,
and praised Govinda with fine gifts and prayers,
and chanted psalms, rang bells and sang his name,
waved lotus garland's offered to the wind,
then went to find their home, safe, pure and new.

From that time on, Yamuna's lake was clear
and free of poisons; sweet as nectar too.
And Krishna came in youthful form to sport
as any human boy is wont to do.

VI. THE BLESSINGS
OF BODY & SOUL

The Maharaj leaned back and smiled and clapped his hands for joy. Tears in his eyes, he gazed upon the sage. "All art springs from redeeméd rage. And Joy's the blossom of the new born Soul. So Krishna holds the world within his arms. And such a telling from his devotee!

Shri Shuka smiled and bowed his head and then looked up again. "Oh gentle king, your words are full of grace. And once the Spirit feeds the Soul, all other hungers are sated as well.

ABOUT THE AUTHOR

Henry C. Timm is a poet and playwright living in Door County, Wisconsin. His poetic works include *Minimal Screeds and Transcendental Scrawls* (2014) and *Learning to See* (2020). Henry received a Masters in Scandinavian Literature from the University of Minnesota, Minneapolis. He began writing poetry and plays while studying at the University of Oslo, Norway. He was a resident playwright at Brandeis University where he worked with Richard Nash.

Henry Timm has taught and directed theater extensively in New England, upstate New York, and Wisconsin, where he ran Dancing Moon Theatre. Henry has written more than a hundred original plays, translations, or adaptations for theater, television and film, including the books and lyrics for more than a dozen full length musicals. He is currently engaged in several works in process: a verse translation of Ibsen's Peer Gynt; Echoes, a series of blank and free verse monologues comprising a kind of modern sequel to The Iliad; and a series of verse adaptations of Krishna stories developed with his son, Radhavallabha Das.